Alchemy of Yeast and Tears

Alchemy of Yeast and Tears

Poems by

Patricia Davis-Muffett

© 2023 Patricia Davis-Muffett. All rights reserved.
This material may not be reproduced in any form, published,
reprinted, recorded, performed, broadcast,
rewritten or redistributed without
the explicit permission of Patricia Davis-Muffett.
All such actions are strictly prohibited by law.

Cover design by Shay Culligan
Cover art by Carroll Muffett
Author photograph by Carroll Muffett

ISBN: 978-1-63980-268-5

Kelsay Books
502 South 1040 East, A-119
American Fork, Utah 84003
Kelsaybooks.com

*for my mother
who taught me anything was possible*

Acknowledgments

I am grateful to the following journals who published some of the poems included here:

Atlanta Review: "Never enough" (first appeared as "Wild Hope")
Best New Poets 2022: "On looking away"
Black Coffee Review: "Counting Breaths"
The Blue Nib Literary Journal: "What we are given"
Bookends Review: "Superpower Wishes"
Comstock Review: "On looking away"
CP Quarterly: "Wild child"
Loch Raven Review: "Beltway with headphones" (first appeared as "Beltway")
Loch Raven Review: "Blood of kindness" (first appeared as "The Labor Ahead")
Neologism: "Night terrors"
ONE ART: a journal of poetry: "What to Do with Your Grief I, II and III"
The Orchards Literary Magazine: "Pruning"
Pretty Owl Poetry: "Dog, watching"
Rat's Ass Review: "On the thirteenth anniversary" (first appeared as "Motherless")
The Raven Review: "As easy as swimming"
The South Shore Review: "Mother Venus"

Heartfelt thanks to all members of my writing groups past and present, to Sarah Ann Winn for her advice on this manuscript, and to Merie Kirby for her advice, feedback and encouragement on this manuscript and many, many poems over the past three decades.

And my deepest gratitude to my family—to my children, who have given me the space to write and have encouraged me to keep going, and to my husband, Carroll Muffett, who has given me encouragement and feedback over our long life together. His beautiful art graces this cover, and I am so lucky that he has always seen me as a poet, even when I struggled to see it myself.

Contents

Pruning	11
Alchemy of yeast and tears	12
Discovery	13
What to do with your grief I	14
Never enough	15
Blood of kindness	16
Mother Venus	18
Counting breaths	20
To friends who waited for me on the other side	21
Spell for my mother	22
What to do with your grief II	23
On looking away	24
Superpower wishes	26
Night terrors	28
On the thirteenth anniversary	30
Wild child	32
Song for Cassiopea	33
The wyvern mother	35
Necessary magic	36
What to do with your grief III	39
Beltway with headphones	40
The elephant mother	41
As easy as swimming	42
Dog, watching	43
What we are given	44

Pruning

My mother and grandfather
fed us all summer,
walked out the door,
returned, arms full
of fist-sized gems.

Always, I forget to
                      water
    weed
                            pick
        at the right time.
A friend, expert gardener,
comes to my yard to talk.

I show her my pride—
the forest of tomato plants
for once, amazingly alive.
Loving their wildness,
I ask her what she thinks.

Spreading one wide frond
across her slim, flat hand,
she says I have to choose
between this wildness
and the fruit I crave.
      See where it is branching—
      here, a whole new plant begins.
Help the plant conserve its energy.
Use it to make more yellow blooms.
Prune here.
It doesn't know
another stem
will make it weaker.
Cut, breathe in the scent
so you can have abundance later.

Alchemy of yeast and tears

My mother died ten days before my last child was born.
> *When you survey the kitchen and find the fruit rotting, get the blender. Peel thin brown skin from the banana, cut rot from mango, pick through desiccated berries. Add ice and yogurt. Blend a miracle.*

If I touch your naked cheek with my ungloved hand, can I read your mind?
> *When you find yourself in a dry county in Kentucky and your new family has wound you up, take a detour on your way to Wal-Mart, cross the state line and accept the dusty grape juice offered when you order a glass of wine.*

Where on my children's bodies will the mark of my decisions show?
> *Once I worked with a man who just stopped coming to work. It took the company nine months to fire him. He died years later believing he knew more than his doctors.*

Does the alabaster fish know she is a lamp?
> *Be careful making bread. The alchemy of yeast and tears makes the rising unpredictable.*

Discovery

A new planet circles our sun
and we are helpless before it,
watching as its atmosphere clears and clouds,
brewing with life and fire.

A near constellation, I contemplate
my appearance from the surface,
the way my glimmerings and dark pockets
will be traced. Will I be Medea or Demeter
or some new myth, unique to this terrain?

Try as I might to reconfigure,
I am fixed in this design.
All that is left is to rise
in this child's southern sky
and to set as his orbit demands.

What to do with your grief I

Butter. Sugar. Flour. Salt.
I am doing what I know.

Nineteen, I call my mother crying:
I can't make the pie crust work.
                              Come home, she says. *We'll fix it.*

The ice in the water,
the fork used to mix,
the way she floured the board.

It's chemistry, yes—
but also this:
the things you have to pass
from hand to hand.

Never enough

Built for grace in water, the leatherback travels
10,000 miles of freezing ocean, hauls
her thousand pounds ashore, trudges
to the space where massive flippers dig
with the fury of a mother who knows her eggs
are desired by dogs, plovers, ghost crabs,
monitors, coatis—creatures who agree on little else.
Her midnight excavation watched
by rangers, pilgrims. She is the only living
species in her genus, *Dermochelys*.

80 eggs laid, plus 30 unfertilized, her offering
to predators. She knows the evidence she leaves:
her weight, her strain. Before returning to
her ocean home, she wastes a precious hour,
gyroscopes across the sand, spinning the illusion
of phantom nests, before hauling herself to sea.

By day, she follows jellyfish, waiting
for their rise up the water column every evening.
She shears them with her perfect scissor jaws—
trying to avoid the masquerade of delicately dancing
ocean plastics, castoffs that will thwart her body's task.

In danger half a century, she ventures far from city lights,
moving nests in search of space to plant her hope,
spiraling through time and loss and current,
never knowing if her work will be enough.

Blood of kindness

A pregnant belly invites the hands of strangers
groping in grocery aisles, triggering
nostalgia for long labors, war stories,
poured out in wistful tone
at the feet of new arrivals to our alien land.

I forgo the tales of
first labor, second, third—
plant a seed instead for later:
> *at 5 months, maybe 6,*
> > *you will look down*
> > > *realize this being must come out.*

When you have panicked well,
open my unwritten book—
talk of water, its gift of weightless labor;
evening primrose oil, squeezed from seeds
from the showy yellow weed—
sundrop, King's cure-all, fever plant—
to thin the veil between your child and the world;
raspberry leaf tea, the "woman's herb,"
discovered by the gods upon Mount Ida,
its fruit's juice, the blood of kindness,
its brambles keeping evil out.
This tea gives strength for what's ahead,
the thrum from your core
pushing child toward air.

But for now
read your books,
paint the room,
get the crib.

It will come: the 3 a.m. call.
Only then can you hear.
For now, we will wait
hidden in darkness and whispers.

Mother Venus

You hover above the meadow
as I pull my robe around me,
shift from bare foot to foot
impatient for the dogs.

You wait on the mornings
when my mind swirls with lists
when I have found myself awake
at one, at three, at five,
ordering and reordering tasks.
You wait on days when I am empty,
when I have nothing to give,
when the pen will not stay in my grip,
when I cannot imagine lifting a dish,
when I struggle to think of the sentences
that must be said—later, later.

Maybe, you are nothing but patience,
goddess of love and beauty,
hanging low in the morning sky.
Your year, foreshortened by five months,
but your day—exhausting, nearly nine months
from the sun rising in the west
to the next sunrise,
more than four Earth months
of toxic night—your desert surface
867 degrees, your atmospheric clouds
thick with sulphuric acid.
But every Earth day, mother star,
as your volcanoes erupt,
as you endure that long, hot night,
you are here to greet me,
usher me into this day—

no matter what awaits,
and on your surface,
some microorganism struggles to survive
sending phosphane gas into the universe—
desperate signal—you're more than meets the eye.

The dogs return, and I whisper my goodbye to you,
looking for your faint shadows
as I feed these animals, put away the dishes,
scrub my face, and muster the smile
that will lure my children from their sleep.

Counting breaths

Maybe you never outgrow
the feeling of lying in bed, waiting
for your mother's return, the moment
her waxy lips brush your forehead,
engulfing you in the boozy perfume
of an evening away.

I stand at my child's crib
and the sleep I assumed dreamless
is troubled by some demon.
He whimpers, pants—
and I am there
to smooth away the world.

How long will this last?
How long will he remember
the scent of me entering his room,
returning to my spot above him.
I count his breaths and revel
in this short-lived power
to answer my child's prayer.

To friends who waited for me on the other side

Forgive me. It was hard to see anything from the bottom—anything, that is, except the blue veins of dying trees breaking through slick dirt walls, distant sky above, North Star taunting, a hunting owl blotting its glow. How could I forget you, waiting, as always—blanket spread, fireflies twinkling around you? You never learned the word 'impatience.' I promise to find footholds, break my nails if necessary, drag myself toward surface. There I'll find your embarrassment of calm, allowing me to strip down to what you've always seen and join you in the pink-tinged garden under the eye of the fading moon.

Spell for my mother

Here, at the end of
chemicals that almost kill you
knives and lasers slicing flesh,
radiation, herbs, pills, potions,
meditation, yoga, prayer—
here, please find this spell.

Gather up your elements.
A rock that fits your palm—
one to smooth against
the worrying of fingers
over months and years.
A fragrant stem, tomato,
its scent of summer,
rows my mother planted—
any nightshade will suffice.
A recent piece of clothing.
Something glowing—
a candle or a cell phone light.

Rise in the hour between three and four.
No need to set alarms. You are awake already.
Strip off your clothes. You won't need them
where you're headed. Enclose yourself in darkness,
a place where you cannot be found—
the bottom of a closet, caressed by silk and wool;
the tiled floor of shower, door or curtain shut.
Ignite your bit of light,
create a pool around your body.
Break the stem of nightshade, so alive
(no matter if you've lost your sense of smell).
Slow your heartbeat, close your eyes,
breathe it in.

What to do with your grief II

9/11. Child dropped at preschool.
Traffic grinds to a halt near the White House.
A plane overhead. The Pentagon burning.
The long trek home to reclaim our child.
We are told to stay in. I venture out.
Blueberries to make a pie.

My mother, so sick. She isn't hungry.
For a time, she is tempted with cookies and pie.
I keep bringing them long after taste has left.

On looking away

If you sit on the couch, with your mother at your side,
her head in a silk scarf, hiding white stubble—
if she holds the Book of Common Prayer, the Bible,
the navy blue 1982 Hymnal containing her favorite songs,
you can always pretend she has not been planning
her funeral, is not trying to give you the chance
to say whatever is stuck in your throat, is not telling you
to brace yourself for what is coming—faster
than either of you imagined.

She lists the psalms, the order of lessons.
Hums her favorite hymns, rehearsing, preparing.
Two weeks and you will put her plans in place.

Instead, you can memorize the pattern
of the ivy-covered rug, the flowers intertwined,
you can search the glass-fronted cabinet
full of Hummel children—the ones she has labeled
under their feet, one for each grandchild, even the one
here in your belly, unusually quiet in his floating almost life today.

You can tell yourself that something will occur—
the *deus ex machina* you have begged for these long months,
the one you offered everything for—all your chips to the middle:
"Here, take years from me, my left hand, my unborn child."
None of it enough.

Instead of speaking, you can kneel at her feet,
offer to clip her toenails, the ones she can't reach,
the one thing she won't ask of her husband
who has looked in her eyes, held her hand
in the infusion room, in the hospital,
at the funeral parlor, with the hospice team.

You can do this one thing you hope says to her
what sticks in your throat is the howl
of love, the howl of despair.

Superpower wishes

Perhaps I am not who I think—
the one who would wish
to disappear before your eyes,
appear somewhere else.
What I want is the power
to stretch time,
cheat death,
be always beside you,
throw wide the doors
and walk through.

But then, there is the task of planting lilacs
and I recall my 6-year-old self
hidden in the stand of sweetness
perched on the metal lid:
LEVITTOWN—the septic tank.
Oblivious and still.

Nine years flying coast to coast,
five hours in limbo each time,
the calm as I settled in my seat,
cabin door closed.
A portal to no time,
the clock turning back:
a book, a pen, a glass.

Teleportation would have stolen
the time beside my mother
as she drove me to countless dance classes
after working two jobs and cooking dinner—
and what of our penniless honeymoon,
driving ourselves across plains into mountains—
silence, music, our own private humor.

And later, kids in the backseat,
what they've revealed
as my eyes watched the road.

Night terrors

There is no way to prepare you—
the way you will be able
to lift a car despite your weakness,
the way you will throw yourself
into the street to snatch your child back,
the way your body will turn
when you fall forward carrying that small body,
twist, resist the impulse to break your fall.
You will hold the baby close, wrench your back.
It will never be the same.

Those things are true
but there is also this—
the wails at two a.m.,
the recognition you'll have
for teenagers who abandon babies
in public bathrooms, walk away;
the jealousy for those
whose time and money
is their own;
the loneliness
        loneliness
                loneliness
when the work is done
when it is too late.
You cannot reach anyone.

The person you were will die.
I hope the new one is strong,
fierce enough to survive.
I hope she will be content
to lay down next to a sleepy child
sing the same lying song,
promising pleasant dreams
though she sees night terrors lurking
just the other side of dusk.

On the thirteenth anniversary

Some years, I have left the calendar
on July—a perpetual 31st—
not wanting to see the month of August come.

Usually, we mark the day
only with a call or text—
we two who loved her most:
only daughter; late life love.
Though in the end,
you loved her most fully,
escorted her
down that dark path
as far as you could go.

Whether I turn the page or not,
the day will come—eyes open
then squeezing shut.
Let it be tomorrow
when I am just the motherless daughter
and not the one who is losing her again.

This thirteenth year
I will gather my children
set a beautiful table
use her wedding china
her mother's crystal.
I will fill vases—
daisies, yellow roses—
I will serve shrimp cocktail,
put ice cubes in wine.
We will end with cookies stuffed with chocolate chips,
butter pecan straight from the box.

We'll lay out photo albums built
one paper corner at a time,
spread Broadway playbills
over the tablecloth she embroidered,
alternate singing showtunes and hymns.

When dark settles,
we will take off our shoes,
process into the yard
cool grass between our toes.
One by one,
we'll step into the garden
sifting rich black dirt
between our fingers
breathe in tomatoes,
newly pruned.
Let the fireflies whirl—
usher out this day.

Wild child

It took a moment before I could turn—
slide on black ice, answering spin across highway
in the thankfully empty dawn. Wheels over ceiling
slowing from seconds to minutes to hours.
I hesitate, not wanting to turn my head.

Still, years later, I flush with relief—
stunned open eyes, shards of glass in hair,
all three, miraculously whole.
You, middle child, sitting under mangled metal
too small to be crushed by crumpled car.

Now fourteen. I hold my hands out,
cupping whatever morsel you seek—
luring your wild animal self
to inch closer as I pretend indifference.

Since birth, I wondered how long I could hold you.
The lump under skin, easily removed.
The friend. a poor secret-keeper,
who opened the black box of your cutting,
letting me walk inside.

This is the part you cannot comprehend:
I have lost you again and again.
Like every young mother,
watching their infant,
willing those lungs:
"Breathe."

Song for Cassiopea

for Kaden, marine biologist

As a child, you were nothing but stalk—
polyp form emerging, latching onto nearby structures,
your body neither male nor female, still you create
clones, proliferate in mangrove swamps—
too warm for many, too polluted—
you are easy in that way.

Leaving polyp form, you are medusa,
telltale bell and arms but no platonic ideal,
moons backlit in aquaria.
Among your jelly peers,
you seem confused, pulsating
upside down, elaborate tendril arms
forever seeking.

Swimmers who know are not afraid.
Your sting is mild—not like the man o' war—
but you hold a secret. Under stress,
you will release your stinging cells, tiny bombs
awaiting prey, distant from your rococo limbs
pretending to be coral.

My child, future scientist, picked you of all creatures
to investigate—after navigating stinging waters of school,
carrying a body mischosen by fate. Unlovable jellies—
bane of bathers, enemy of engineers, useless
nuisance, beauty of the deep.

Now, this child, transitioned,
buries himself in science, studies
how you protect yourself,
disappearing so easily—
thinner than a contact lens.

I see you stretching back into Cambrian fossils,
doing the hard work of evolution, organizing cells
into your chosen bodies, accomplishing
miraculous survival.

The wyvern mother

The lost little boy in your novel—
the one you wrote all that long year
after switching schools with
your little brother, to protect him
when, like clockwork, he
burst into tears, threw chairs—
wandered into the cold mouth
of cave, transformed into dragon.
His sister, full of magic,
followed, quickly found him.

The boy, though, was content
to retain his wyvern form.
His sister stayed, shielded him from evil,
tried to coax him to revert to human shape.

Their mother knew only
both her children were gone.
In their absence, she grew
weak and sick, as mothers do
in stories, while her children
cast spells, reveled
in scales and fire,
explored deeper and deeper
into earth and rock
forgetting their plan
to ascend
to shocking sun.

Necessary magic

                Food   stuck   pots,
      clothes strewn floor,
paint   Legos
      spilled

Piece by piece,
           she takes it on—
not the kind of clean
      in houses ever-prepped for guests—
the kind that makes it possible
to go on with your life.

                        Heavy sleeper as a child—
                  dreaming as a tree fell on the roof,
            scraped its long way down,
        beyond her wall,
            tearing shingles in its wake—

she became the one whose body rose
        from deepest sleep to need in darkness—
            comfort, food or terror.

She, the one who whisked
the gagging child to the bathroom,
knelt beside him,
rag soaked in ice
on forehead,
no flick of light,
stripped the sweat-soaked bed,
found softest well-worn sheets,
carried child once again to bed,
incanted, hummed and lulled
willing white blood cells
to do their worst,
return the child to health.

Seeming lifetime
scraping pots and pans,
stripping beds
cooling fevers,

       sleeplessness
               wakefulness

the task to come:
her small boy
bashed his head
against the bricks
cried out
      I don't want to live.

She calls the doctors,
those who put her on a list,
as her child slowly dimmed.

Find the one who'll see them,
sit quiet as her child bends
to doctor's spell,
                      vipers
                                             toads
       insects
spilling from his mouth:

he frightened me
he touched me
hands around my throat

She wills the room
to stop its spin
keeps her body still,
incants a spell
to make her heartbeat slow.

What to do with your grief III

for Dionne, in the wake of George Floyd's murder

Today, Minneapolis burns
and sparks catch fire in New York,
Atlanta, here in DC.
Your voice says
what I know but cannot know:

> *This is my fear every time they leave me.*

Three beautiful sons, brilliant, alive.

I do what my mother taught me.
Butter. Sugar. Flour. Salt.
I bring this to you.
This work of my hands.
This piece of my day.
I am doing what I know.

Beltway with headphones

From the sullen teenage silence:
"There are people in all these cars.
Maybe that one in the silver Honda
just filed for divorce.
Maybe the black sedan has cancer."
I play along: *"Maybe the Focus*
carries a mourner, eyes red from crying.
Maybe the hatchback—
a new baby, parents
terrified with wonder."

Silence settles except
the road noise
click of turn signal
and the howl of every person
on this stretch of highway
shaking the car until
we have no choice
but to listen to their cries.

The elephant mother

The elephant mother dances her grief,
touching her soles to the stillborn child,
waltzing alone for three dark days.

Then, the time for pilgriming,
return to land where mothers and sisters
turn to bones and bones.

How could she dance?
Her child is dead.
How can she face this decay?

The matriarchs move from the herd.
They do not sound their trumpeted grief,
slowly swing their massive heads.

The matriarchs scan their leaderless herd
for those who will grieve their bones.

As easy as swimming

Seventeen long months, this child grows,
learning her mother's voice
as she searches, tireless,
for the dwindling salmon.

Finally, the calf emerges, swims.
No more than thirty minutes—
she is gone. The child, imagined, hoped-for,
the future of a dwindling breed.

What was it that made her
keep the vigil, risk herself,
to keep this child afloat seventeen long days,
1000 miles, nudging her toward air?

Was she convinced
she could save her child
make her whole again—this being
she loved already, as it slipped from sea to sea?

Those nine long months I carried you
as my mother slipped away.
Laboring in water, my head beneath the surface
as I fought the urge to scream.

Finally, your whole self in the world,
no matter my imperfect carrying.
Here you are, the rush of love immediate.
I would do anything to buoy you toward air.

Thirteen years. Still miraculous, alive.
This summer, that orca mother
carries another calf. As if this is
as easy as swimming, she continues.

Dog, watching

Cursing the dog at five a.m.,
darkness clutching its final hour,
bare feet on wooden stairs
the tendons of my ankles short
barely seeing the next stair down.
The puppy waits at the edge of the stairs
to see if I will venture
into wet grass, dark—

I take the step to show it's safe
wonder if my feet will meet
a rodent killed, a slug unfurled,
deer droppings from the night before.
No matter what, I know
I can show no hesitation.
She is watching me,
learning to gauge
the danger of the world.

For now, the world is just
this grass between my toes,
owl hooting from the treetops,
sun glowing on horizon,
night relinquishing its grasp.
Let's just let the truth
reveal itself in time.

What we are given

The rain. The weeds.
The rough dismissal.
The restless dog.

My youngest child, the one who has lived the least,
been handed the greatest suffering,
fights sleep like it will take his soul.
Last night, he wandered the house at 3 a.m.,
switching on lights, waking the dog,
building me a house in his virtual world.

He asks me to choose—
what wood, what stone, what trees?
He makes houses for everyone,
but others are granted fewer options.
For me, he reserves the largest lot,
fills it with the flowers I love—
lilacs and daisies and poppies
bursting from the virtual lawn.

I met his love with exhaustion.
Today, I vow to offer
my disappointing self,
wrapped in this blanket,
watching this rain,
tending this garden.
I hope it is enough.

About the Author

Patricia Davis-Muffett holds a Master of Fine Arts from the University of Minnesota. Her work has appeared widely in literary journals in print and online and has won numerous honors including a Best of the Net nomination, inclusion in Best New Poets 2022, second place in the 2022 Joe Gouveia OuterMost Poetry Contest, judged by Marge Piercy and first honorable mention in the same competition in 2021, honorable mention in Comstock Review's 2021 Muriel Craft Bailey Memorial Contest, and finalist in the 2020 Julia Darling Poetry Prize. She has taught English and Creative Writing in the past, but she now makes her living in technology marketing. She lives with her husband, children, two dogs, and one cat in Rockville, Maryland.

Made in the USA
Middletown, DE
15 March 2023